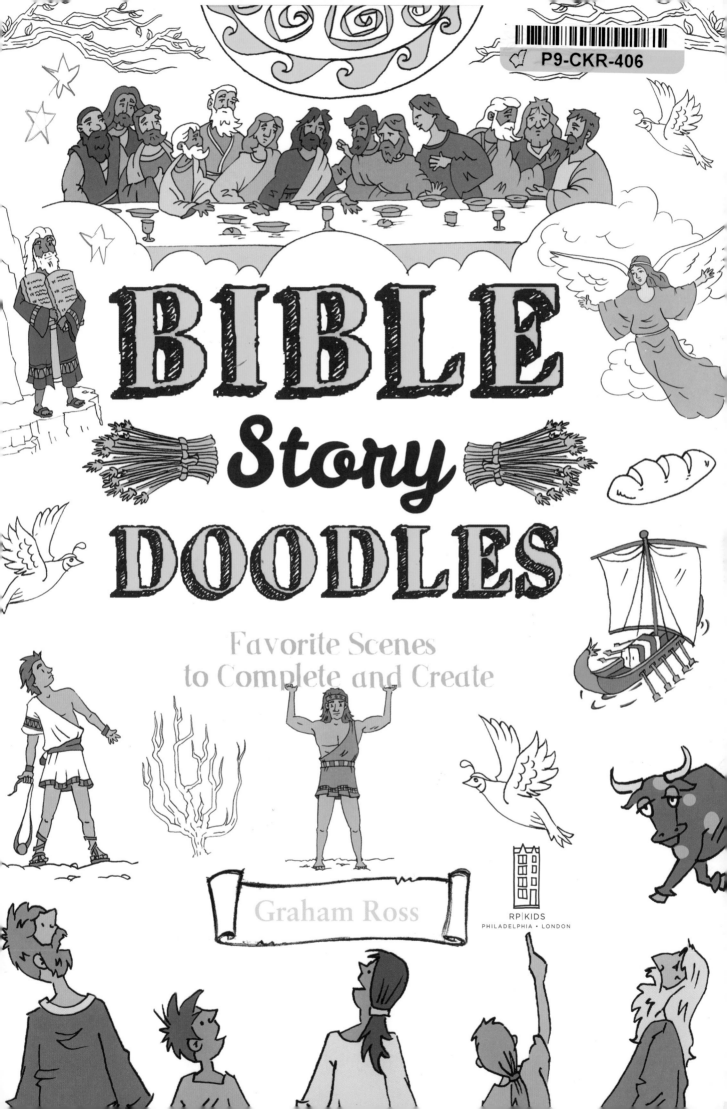

BIBLE Story DOODLES

Favorite Scenes to Complete and Create

Graham Ross

RP|KIDS
PHILADELPHIA · LONDON

First published in Great Britain in 2014 by Buster Books, an imprint of
Michael O'Mara Books Limited, 9 Lion Yard, Tremadoc Road, London SW4 7NQ.

First published in the United States by Running Press Book Publishers, 2014

Printed in China

Books published by Running Press are available at special discounts for bulk purchases in the
United States by corporations, institutions, and other organizations. For more information, please
contact the Special Markets Department at the Perseus Books Group, 2300 Chestnut
Street, Suite 200, Philadelphia, PA 19103, or call (800) 810-4145, ext. 5000,
or e-mail special.markets@perseusbooks.com.

ISBN 978-0-7624-5217-0

9 8 7 6 5 4 3 2
Digit on the right indicates the number of this printing

This edition published by:
Running Press Kids
An Imprint of Running Press Book Publishers
A Member of the Perseus Books Group
2300 Chestnut Street
Philadelphia, PA 19103–4371

Visit us on the web!
www.runningpress.com/kids

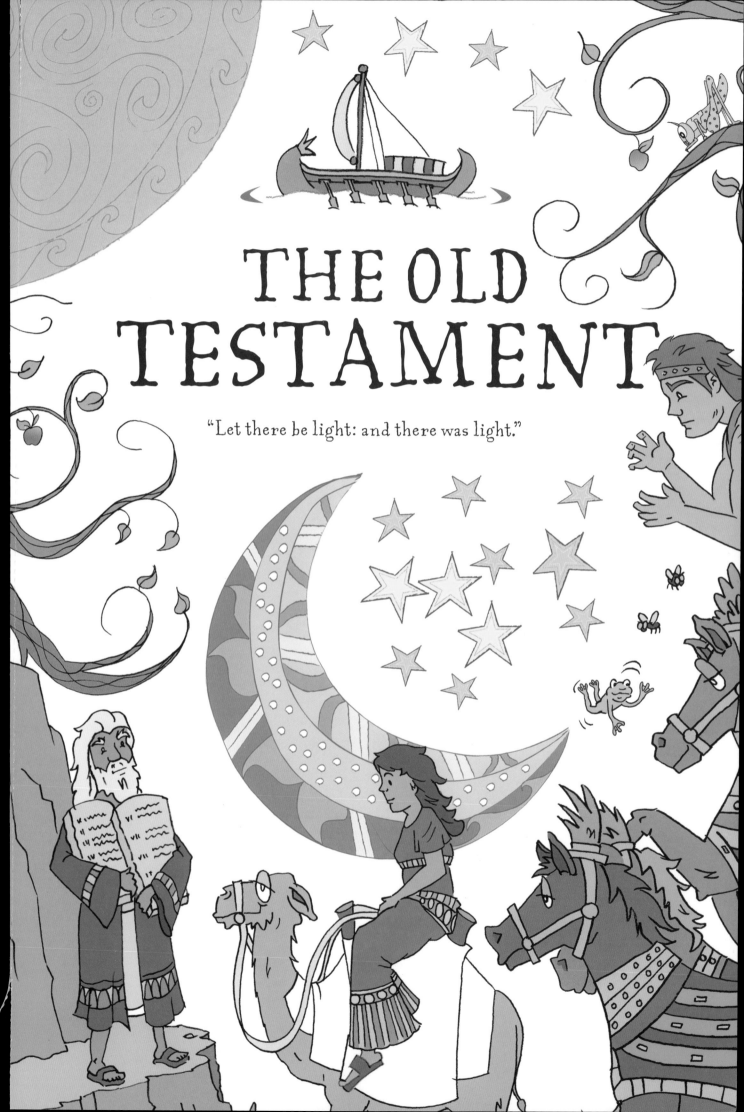

THE OLD TESTAMENT

"Let there be light: and there was light."

Add more waves to the sea
and clouds to the sky.

GENESIS 1

And God said, "Let the
waters under the heaven
be gathered together
unto one place . . ."

GENESIS 1

"Let the earth bring forth grass, the herb yielding seed, and the fruit tree yielding fruit..."

Draw amazing plants sprouting from the earth.

Doodle more stars between the sun and moon.

GENESIS 1

And God made two great lights; the greater light to rule the day, and the lesser light to rule the night: he made the stars also.

GENESIS 1

And God created
great whales, and
every living creature
that moveth...

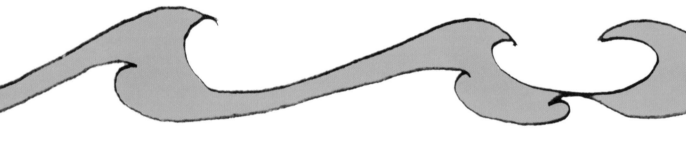

Draw more flying birds and super sea creatures.

GENESIS 1

And God said, "Let us make man in our image, after our likeness..."

Draw people alongside these animals.

Add more fruit and leaves to the tree of knowledge.

GENESIS 2

And out of the ground made the Lord God to grow every tree that is pleasant to the sight, and good for food . . .

So he drove out the man; and he placed at the east of the garden of Eden Cherubims, and a flaming sword which turned every way, to keep the way of the tree of life.

Draw the tree of life.

Add red-hot flames to the sword.

How many sheep are in Abel's flock?

And the Lord had respect unto Abel and to his offering: But unto Cain and to his offering he had not respect.

And the Lord set a mark upon Cain, lest any finding him should kill him.

Draw the mark of Cain.

The animals went in two by two! Copy each animal so that they are all traveling in pairs.

GENESIS 7

And they went in unto Noah into the ark, two and two of all flesh, wherein is the breath of life.

Fill Noah's ark with amazing animals.

GENESIS 9

"I do set my bow
in the cloud, and it
shall be for a token of
a covenant between
me and the earth."

Decorate the sky with a colorful rainbow.

GENESIS 11

Build the tower of Babel.

And they said, "Go to, let us build us a city and a tower, whose top may reach unto heaven ..."

Decorate the angels on their way to Sodom and Gomorrah.

GENESIS 19

And there came two angels to Sodom at even . . .

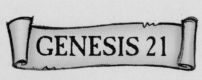

GENESIS 21

What are Hagar and Ishmael taking into the desert?

And Abraham rose up early in the morning, and took bread, and a bottle of water, and gave it unto Hagar...

Draw the massive mountain in Moriah.

GENESIS 22

"Take now thy son, thine only son Isaac, whom thou lovest, and get thee into the land of Moriah; and offer him there for a burnt offering upon one of the mountains which I will tell thee of."

What is caught in the thicket?

And Abraham lifted up his eyes, and looked, and behold behind him a ram caught in a thicket by his horns . . .

Give the camels bright and bold patterns.

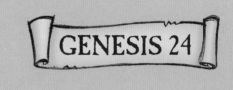

And when she had done giving him drink, she said, "I will draw water for thy camels also, until they have done drinking."

And he dreamed, and behold a ladder set up on the earth, and the top of it reached to heaven: and behold the angels of God ascending and descending on it.

Complete Jacob's ladder and draw more astonishing angels.

Finish the fun designs on Joseph's coat of many colors.

GENESIS 37

Now Israel loved Joseph more than all his children, because he was the son of his old age: and he made him a coat of many colors.

GENESIS 37

"For, behold, we were binding sheaves in the field, and, lo, my sheaf arose, and also stood upright; and, behold, your sheaves stood round about, and made obeisance to my sheaf."

Show other sheaves of corn bowing
down to Joseph's sheaf.

Draw the sun, moon, and eleven stars in Joseph's dream.

And he dreamed yet another dream, and told it his brethren, and said, "Behold, I have dreamed a dream more; and, behold, the sun and the moon and the eleven stars made obeisance to me."

And the chief butler told his dream to Joseph, and said to him, "In my dream, behold, a vine was before me..."

Doodle juicy bunches of grapes and the Pharaoh's cup.

When the chief baker saw that the interpretation was good, he said unto Joseph, "I also was in my dream, and, behold, I had three white baskets on my head..."

Doodle three baskets balancing on top of the baker's head.

GENESIS 41

And it came to pass at the end of two full years, that Pharaoh dreamed . . .

Finish the Pharaoh's dream so that there
are seven skinny cows and seven fattened cows.

GENESIS 44

Hide a silver cup in Benjamin's bag.

And he searched, and
began at the eldest, and
left at the youngest:
and the cup was found
in Benjamin's sack.

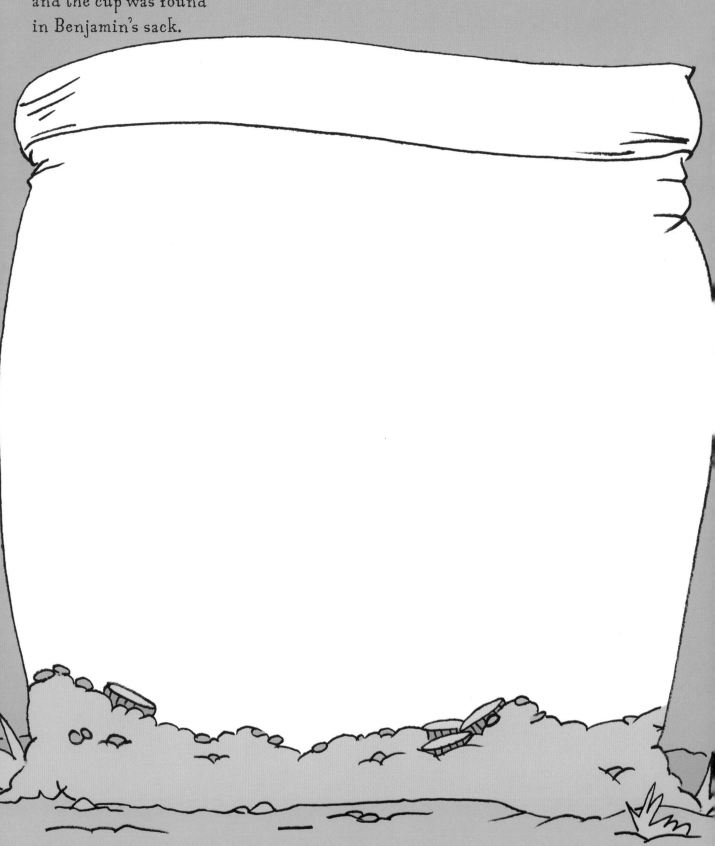

Swaddle baby Moses in the basket.

And when she could not longer hide him, she took for him an ark of bulrushes, and daubed it with slime and with pitch, and put the child therein; and she laid it in the flags by the river's brink.

Cover the bush in red-hot flames . . .

. . . and draw the serpent writhing in the dust.

EXODUS 3

And the angel of the Lord appeared unto him in a flame of fire out of the midst of a bush: and he looked, and, behold, the bush burned with fire, and the bush was not consumed.

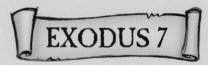

EXODUS 7

"Take thy rod, and stretch out thine hand upon the waters of Egypt, upon their streams, upon their rivers, and upon their ponds, and upon all their pools of water, that they may become blood . . ."

Sail more boats on the river of blood.

EXODUS 8

"Let my people go, that they may serve me. And if thou refuse to let them go, behold, I will smite all thy borders with frogs."

EXODUS 8

Create a cloud of buzzing flies.

"Else, if thou wilt not let
my people go, behold, I
will send swarms of flies
upon thee, and upon
thy servants, and upon
thy people, and into thy
houses: and the houses
of the Egyptians shall be
full of swarms of flies,
and also the ground
whereon they are."

Perch more locusts on the branch.

And the locusts went up over all the land of Egypt, and rested in all the coasts of Egypt...

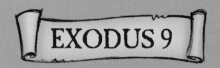

EXODUS 9

And Moses stretched
forth his rod toward
heaven: and the Lord
sent thunder and hail,
and the fire ran along
upon the ground; and
the Lord rained hail
upon the land of Egypt.

Let the lightning bolts and heavy
hail fall from these stormy clouds.

EXODUS 11

And the Lord said unto Moses, "Yet will I bring one plague more upon Pharaoh, and upon Egypt; afterwards he will let you go hence . . ."

EXODUS 14

And the children of Israel went into the midst of the sea upon the dry ground: and the waters were a wall unto them on their right hand, and on their left.

Make way for Moses and his people
by parting the walls of water.

EXODUS 16

Then said the Lord unto Moses, "Behold, I will rain bread from heaven for you..."

Draw more quail in the sky . . .

. . . and more bread on the ground.

EXODUS 20

Fill the sky with thunder and lightning.

And all the people saw
the thunderings, and
the lightnings...

Fill the page with gold jewelry.

EXODUS 32

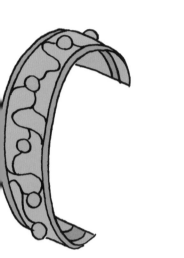

And Aaron said unto them, "Break off the golden earrings, which are in the ears of your wives, of your sons, and of your daughters, and bring them unto me."

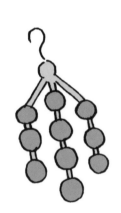

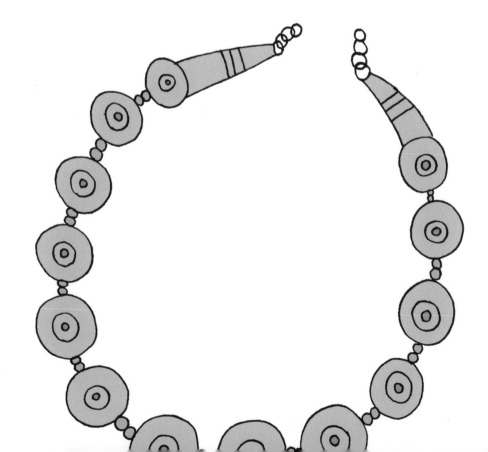

NUMBERS 14

"If the Lord delight in us, then he will bring us into this land, and give it us; a land which floweth with milk and honey."

Plant plenty of vegetables and add buzzing bees around the hives.

Provide trumpets for the priests to play . . .

So the people shouted when the priests blew with the trumpets: and it came to pass, when the people heard the sound of the trumpet, and the people shouted with a great shout, that the wall fell down flat . . .

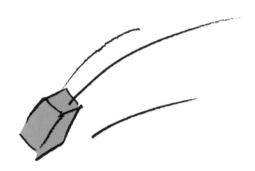

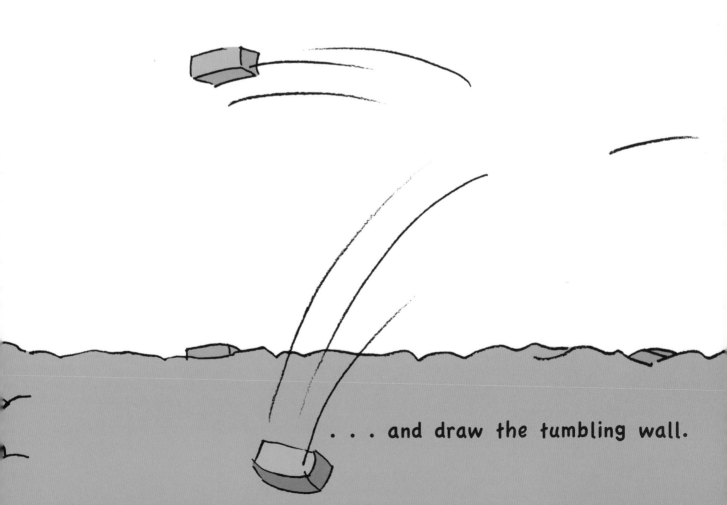

. . . . and draw the tumbling wall.

JUDGES 14

What is Samson about to fight?

Then went Samson down, and his father and his mother, to Timnath, and came to the vineyards of Timnath: and, behold, a young lion roared against him.

JUDGES 14

How strong is Samson?

And the spirit of the
Lord came mightily
upon him...

Give Samson a haircut.

"...If I be shaven, then my strength will go from me, and I shall become weak, and be like any other man."

And Samson took
hold of the two middle
pillars upon which
the house stood . . .

Show the temple and pillars that Samson is destroying.

I SAMUEL 4

And when the ark of the covenant of the Lord came into the camp, all Israel shouted with a great shout, so that the earth rang again.

Decorate the ark of the covenant.

I SAMUEL 10

Hide Saul in a pile of bags.

And the Lord
answered, "Behold,
he hath hid himself
among the stuff."

Build a sacrificial fire for Saul to light.

And Saul said,
"Bring hither a burnt
offering to me, and
peace offerings."

I SAMUEL 17

And there went out
a champion out of the
camp of the Philistines,
named Goliath, of
Gath, whose height was
six cubits and a span.

How tall is the giant?

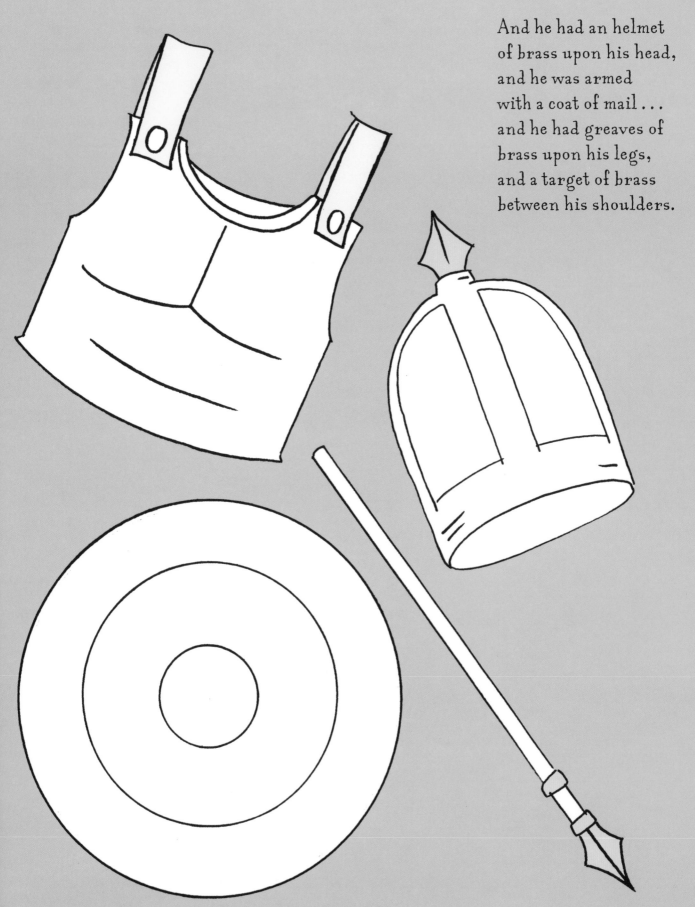

And he had an helmet of brass upon his head, and he was armed with a coat of mail ... and he had greaves of brass upon his legs, and a target of brass between his shoulders.

Decorate Goliath's armor.

I SAMUEL 19

And Michal took an image, and laid it in the bed, and put a pillow of goats' hair for his bolster, and covered it with a cloth.

What has Michal hidden under the covers?

Match the design on Saul's coat to the cloth in David's hand.

"Moreover, my father, see, yea, see the skirt of thy robe in my hand: for in that I cut off the skirt of thy robe . . ."

"And now this blessing
which thine handmaid
hath brought unto my
lord, let it even be given
unto the young men
that follow my lord."

Load up Abigail's donkeys with food.

II SAMUEL 18

And Absalom rode upon a mule, and the mule went under the thick boughs of a great oak, and his head caught hold of the oak, and he was taken up between the heaven and the earth; and the mule that was under him went away.

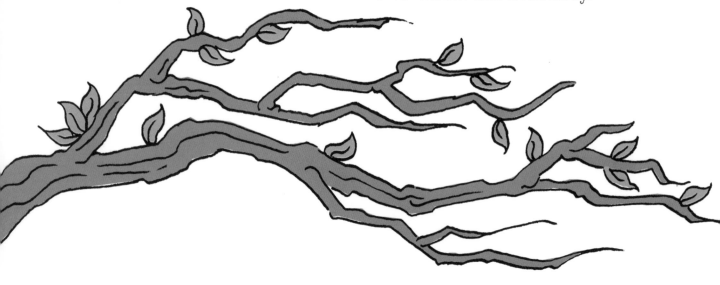

Draw Absalom with his hair caught in the tree branch.

"And, behold, I purpose to build an house unto the name of the Lord my God . . ."

Finish Solomon's Temple.

I KINGS 10

And she came to
Jerusalem with a very
great train, with
camels that bare spices,
and very much gold,
and precious stones...

What is the Queen of Sheba's camel caravan carrying?

I KINGS 17

Show more ravens bringing food to Elijah.

And the ravens brought him bread and flesh in the morning, and bread and flesh in the evening; and he drank of the brook.

Design a chariot of fire to take Elijah up to heaven.

And it came to pass, as they still went on, and talked, that, behold, there appeared a chariot of fire . . .

II KINGS 5

Then went he down, and dipped himself seven times in Jordan, according to the saying of the man of God: and his flesh came again like unto the flesh of a little child, and he was clean.

What else is happening along the river?

ISAIAH 6

Above it stood the seraphims: each one had six wings . . .

Draw the six-winged seraphs in Isaiah's vision.

NEHEMIAH 2

And they said, "Let us rise up and build. So they strengthened their hands for this good work."

Help Nehemiah and his men rebuild Jerusalem
with more blocks of stone.

DANIEL 3

"Lo, I see four men loose, walking in the midst of the fire, and they have no hurt; and the form of the fourth is like the Son of God."

Fit Shadrach, Meshach, and Abednego in the furnace with a mysterious fourth person.

DANIEL 5

In the same hour came forth fingers of a man's hand, and wrote ... upon the plaster of the wall of the king's palace.

Fill Belshazzar's feasting table with cups
and show the spirit's hand writing on the wall.

DANIEL 6

"My God hath sent his angel, and hath shut the lions' mouths, that they have not hurt me."

Complete the den of lions.

JONAH 1

Now the Lord had prepared a great fish to swallow up Jonah.

What's about to gobble up Jonah?

JONAH 1&2

And Jonah was in the belly of the fish three days and three nights.

Then Jonah prayed unto the Lord his God out of the fish's belly . . .

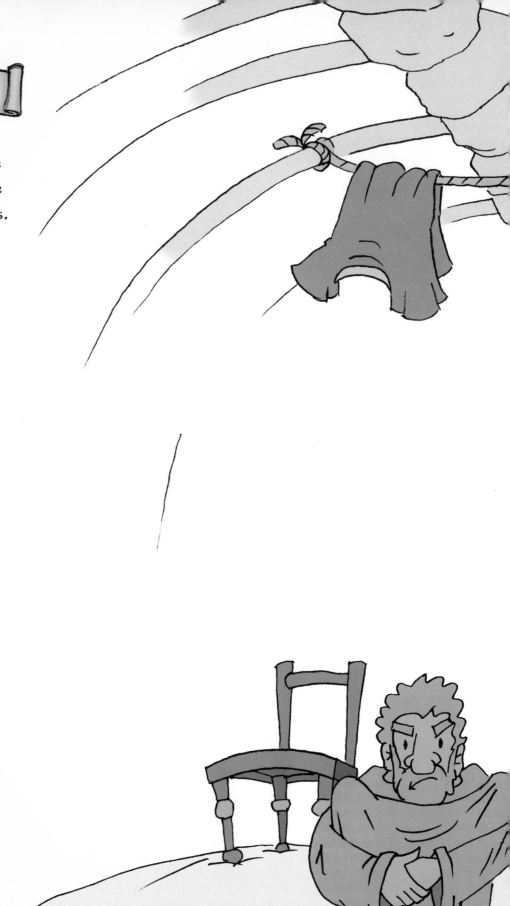

What else has the great fish swallowed?

JONAH 4

And the Lord God prepared a gourd, and made it to come up over Jonah, that it might be a shadow over his head, to deliver him from his grief.

Draw the vine that shelters Jonah from the sun at Nineveh.

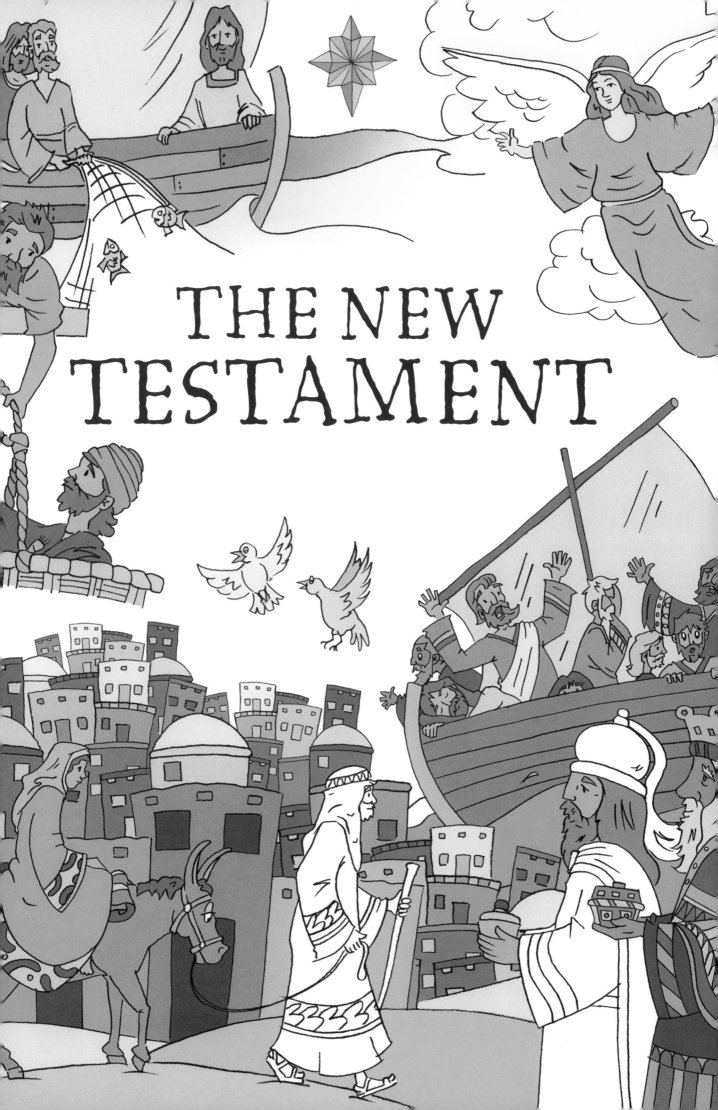

THE NEW TESTAMENT

...Behold, the angel of the Lord appeared unto him in a dream, saying, "Joseph, thou son of David, fear not to take unto thee Mary thy wife..."

What has Joseph made in his workshop?

LUKE 2

And Joseph also went up from Galilee, out of the city of Nazareth, into Judaea, unto the city of David, which is called Bethlehem.

Finish the skyline of Bethlehem.

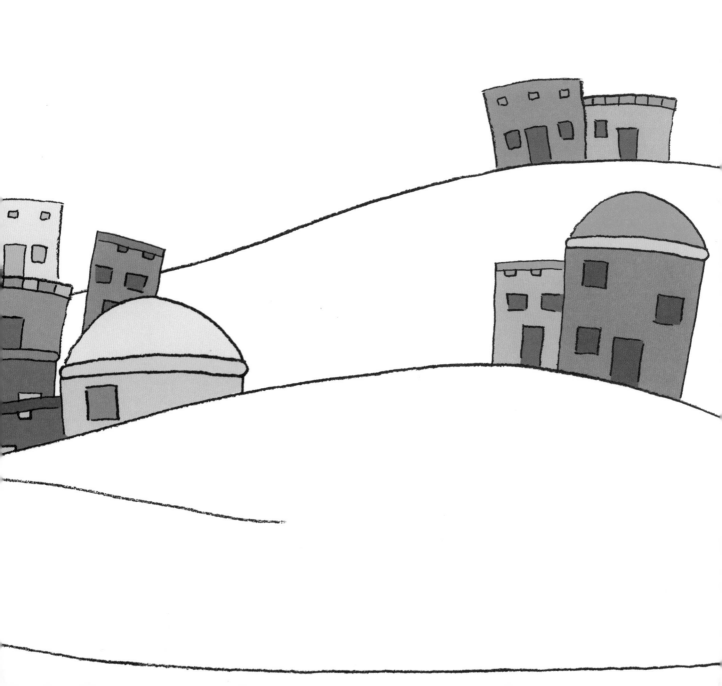

LUKE 2

And she brought forth her first born son, and wrapped him in swaddling clothes, and laid him in a manger; because there was no room for them in the inn.

What animals are watching over Jesus in the stable?

LUKE 2

And the angel said unto them, "Fear not: for, behold, I bring you good tidings of great joy, which shall be to all people."

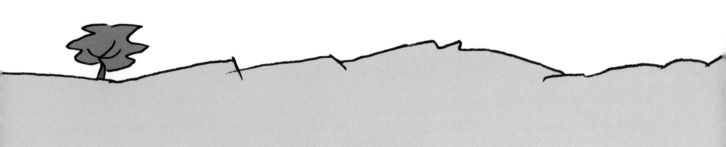

Show more angels visiting the shepherds.

MATTHEW 2

And he sent them to
Bethlehem, and said,
"Go and search
diligently for the
young child . . ."

Decorate the wise men with sparkling jewels and bright patterns.

When they had heard the king, they departed; and, lo, the star, which they saw in the east, went before them, till it came and stood over where the young child was.

Sprinkle more stars in the sky.

And when they had opened their treasures, they presented unto him gifts; gold, and frankincense, and myrrh.

Decorate the boxes of gold, frankincense, and myrrh.

MATTHEW 3

Then went out to him Jerusalem, and all Judaea, and all the region round about Jordan . . .

Draw the spirit of the Lord as a dove.

Then cometh Jesus from Galilee to Jordan unto John, to be baptized of him.

Then was Jesus led up of the Spirit into the wilderness to be tempted of the devil.

What beasts and birds are in the wilderness?

And Jesus, walking by the sea of Galilee, saw two brethren, Simon called Peter, and Andrew his brother, casting a net into the sea: for they were fishers.

MATTHEW 5

And seeing the
multitudes, he went
up into a mountain:
and when he was set,
his disciples came
unto him . . .

Draw a bigger crowd for Jesus to preach to.

MARK 2

And they come unto him, bringing one sick of the palsy . . .

Who is being lowered through the roof?

MATTHEW 7

"Therefore whosoever heareth these sayings of mine, and doeth them, I will liken him unto a wise man, which built his house upon a rock."

Build the wise man's house upon the rock.

MATTHEW 7

"And every one that heareth these sayings of mine, and doeth them not, shall be likened unto a foolish man, which built his house upon the sand."

Build the foolish man's house upon the sand.

"And the rain descended, and the floods came, and the winds blew ..."

Draw heavy raindrops and submerge the foolish man's house underwater.

MATTHEW 8

And, behold, there arose a
great tempest in the sea . . .

Crash huge waves against the boat.

"And when he sowed, some seeds fell by the way side, and the fowls came and devoured them up."

Draw birds eating the scattered seed . . .

MATTHEW 13

"And some fell among thorns; and the thorns sprung up, and choked them."

. . . and thistles choking the corn.

And they did all eat,
and were filled.

Fill the baskets with enough food to feed the people.

MATTHEW 14

And immediately Jesus stretched forth his hand, and caught him, and said unto him, "O thou of little faith, wherefore didst thou doubt?"

Who is saving Peter from drowning?

And when he thus had spoken, he cried with a loud voice, "Lazarus, come forth."

JOHN 11

What is happening in the tomb?

Draw more objects falling to the ground.

"My house shall be called the house of prayer; but ye have made it a den of thieves."

And a very great multitude spread their garments in the way; others cut down branches from the trees, and strawed them in the way.

Cover the ground in clothes and palm leaves.

Now when the even was come, he sat down with the twelve.

Fill the table with food for
Jesus and his disciples.

MATTHEW 26

Then cometh Jesus
with them unto a place
called Gethsemane.

What flowers and plants are in the garden of Gethsemane?

MATTHEW 26

And Peter remembered the word of Jesus, which said unto him, "Before the cock crow, thou shalt deny me thrice." And he went out, and wept bitterly.

Draw the crowing cockerel on the fence.

Draw the symbol of Christ on the hill.

"After three days
I will rise again."

MATTHEW 28

"He is not here:
for he is risen ..."

Draw an angel sitting in the tomb.

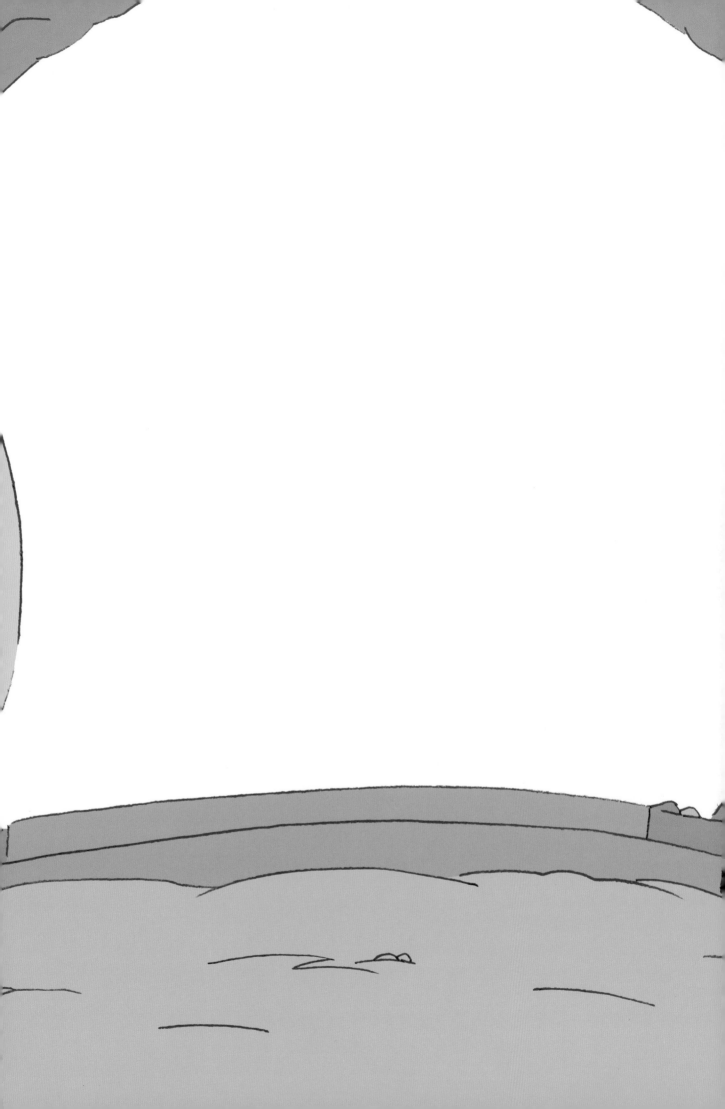

LUKE 24

And it came to pass,
while he blessed them,
he was parted from
them, and carried
up into heaven.

Draw Jesus ascending
into heaven and doodle
more rays of light.

And suddenly there came a sound from heaven as of a rushing mighty wind, and it filled all the house where they were sitting. And there appeared unto them cloven tongues like as of fire, and it sat upon each of them.

Add small flickering flames on top
of the apostles' heads.

ACTS 9

Then the disciples took him by night, and let him down by the wall in a basket.

Draw the rest of the basket to help Saul escape.

What has bitten Paul?

ACTS 28

And when Paul had gathered a bundle of sticks, and laid them on the fire, there came a viper out of the heat, and fastened on his hand.

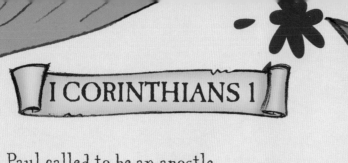

I CORINTHIANS 1

Paul called to be an apostle
of Jesus Christ through
the will of God...

Doodle on Paul's scroll.